NATURE FILES
ANIMAL HOMES

NATURE FILES – ANIMAL HOMES
was produced by

David West ☆☆ Children's Books

7 Princeton Court
55 Felsham Road
London SW15 1AZ

Designer: Julie Joubinaux
Editor: Gail Bushnell
Picture Research: Carlotta Cooper

First published in Great Britain by Heinemann
Library, Halley Court, Jordan Hill, Oxford
OX2 8EJ, part of Harcourt Education.
Heinemann is a registered trademark
of Harcourt Education Ltd.

07 06 05 04 03
10 9 8 7 6 5 4 3 2 1

ISBN 0 431 18245 0 (HB)
ISBN 0 431 18252 3 (PB)

British Library Cataloguing in Publication Data

Anita Ganeri, 1961-
Animal homes. - (Nature files)
1. Animals - Habitations - Juvenile literature
I. Title
591.5'64

PHOTO CREDITS :
Abbreviations: t-top, m-middle, b-bottom, r-right,
l-left, c-centre.

Front cover tl (William Osborn), tr (Tom Vezo), b
(Jeff Foott) - naturepl.com. Pages 3 & 17b (Bruce
Davidson), 4t & 16 (William Osborn), 4b, 25b
(Jurgen Freund), 5t & 18t, 28t (Pete Oxford), 5b
(Paul Hobson), 7b (Warwick Sloss), 8t, 24t, 29bl
(David Kjaer), 8b (Hans Christoph), 8–9 (Brian
Lightfoot), 9 (Bernard Castelein), 10bl (Phil
Chapman), 10br, 12b (Jeff Foott), 12t (Bengt
Lundberg), 19b (Vincent Munier), 13t, 27t
(Lynn Stone), 13b (Andrew Harrington), 14 both
(Premaphotos), 15m (John B. Free), 15b (Martin
Gabriel), 16–17 (Georgette Dowma), 18bl (John
Cancalosi), 18br (Ron O'Connor), 21m (Tim
Martin), 21b (Andrew Cooper), 22b, 23br, 25t
(Constantinos Petrinos), 23bl (Sue Daly), 24b (Albert
Aanensen), 26t (Martin Dohrn), 27b, 28b (Anup
Shah), 29br (Steve Packham) - naturepl.com. 6t (S.J.
Krasemann), 7m (Mark Edwards), 11 (Alain Beignet),
20b (Michal Gunther), 29t (Norbert Wu) - Still
Pictures. 6b, 22t, 23t - Corbis Images. 7t (Brian
Kenney), 10t (Mary Plage), 17t (Adrian Bailey), 20t
(Michael Fogden), 21t (Harry Fox), 26b (David
Thompson) - Oxford Scientific Films. 15t (Justin
Peach), 25m (Carlos Villoch) - Image Quest 3D.

Every effort has been made to contact copyright
holders of any material reproduced in this book. Any
omissions will be rectified in subsequent printings if
notice is given to the publishers.

Printed and bound in Italy

*An explanation of difficult words can be
found in the glossary on page 31.*

NATURE FILES

ANIMAL HOMES

Anita Ganeri

Heinemann LIBRARY

CONTENTS

Tiny insects, called termites, build amazing tower-like nests from clay and mud. A nest the size of this one in Australia can take up to 50 years to build.

Hermit crabs do not have their own shells but use old or cast-off shells as homes instead. When a crab grows too big for one shell, it simply finds a larger one.

INTRODUCTION

From tiny, dusty holes in the ground to extraordinary feats of engineering, animals live in a wide variety of homes both on land and in water. Using materials that range from soil and wood, to wax, saliva and silk, many animals work hard to create safe places, where they can shelter from bad weather, hide from enemies, and raise their young. Some homes are temporary. Every night, apes build a new sleeping nest in the trees. Other homes, such as prairie dog tunnels, are used all year round.

Most species of birds build nests, where they lay their eggs and raise their young. Tiny hummingbirds build delicate, cup-shaped nests from moss, petals, leaves and cobwebs.

A mole surfaces to collect grass and leaves with which to line its underground nest. Moles dig extensive tunnels and chambers in the soil, using their front paws as spades.

Some animals find homes in the natural world around them, such as in caves, holes or trees. Others are skilful builders. Some animals have no fixed home but constantly roam from place to place, looking for water and food.

No FIXED HOME

Rather than having a fixed home, some animals occupy a patch of land, called a territory. Here they find food, mates for breeding and safe places to sleep or rest. They guard their territories closely against intruders.

Bromeliads are rainforest plants which grow in the trees. Rain water collects in pools formed by the overlapping leaves. Some tree frogs use these pools as tadpole nurseries.

Zebras roam the African grasslands. They live in herds which seek food in set home ranges (territories). In the dry season, when food is scarce, the zebras travel hundreds of kilometres.

SETTING UP HOUSE

All around us, there are examples of structures built by people. Some animals are also master builders. They use various techniques to construct homes. The simplest structures are the hard cases which tiny sea creatures, such as coral polyps, build to protect their soft bodies. More complex structures include the elaborate nests built by insects from wax, paper, clay and mud.

Birds' nests are among the best-known animal homes. In spring, many birds collect twigs, moss, leaves and other materials to build their nests.

A kingfisher's territory is a stretch of riverbank which it defends against intruders. It digs a tunnel where it makes its nest and lays its eggs, safe from predators.

A forest destroyed by mining.

Amazing FACT

All over the world, animals' homes are in danger from habitat destruction. The rainforests are home to millions of species of animals, at least half of all animals known to science. Yet the forests are being quickly destroyed, for land and wood. They may disappear completely in 50 years' time.

One of the safest places for an animal to live is a burrow under the ground. Some burrows are simply holes in the ground. Others are networks of tunnels and chambers.

Puffins nest in burrows on steep, grassy cliffs. Inside their burrows, they are safe from attack by gulls.

IN A HOLE

Some animals use their homes as traps to catch prey. A female trapdoor spider digs her burrow in soft ground and lines it with silk. She uses more silk to bind grains of soil to make a circular lid. Then she opens the lid and lies in wait. If an insect walks by, she grabs it, drags it into her burrow and slams the lid shut.

When it is time to lay her eggs, the trapdoor spider ties the lid down from the inside with lines of silk. Then she lays her eggs in safety, in the bottom of her burrow.

A mole's front paws have strong claws for digging. The mole loosens soil with its snout and paws, then uses its body to press the soil against the tunnel walls.

MOLE HILLS

A mole spends most of its life underground in a network of burrows and tunnels. Sometimes it pushes up to the surface, forming a mole hill. This allows air to filter down to the tunnels. Below ground, there are chambers for sleeping, nesting and for storing earthworms – the mole's main food.

Gerbil in the Thar desert, India.

Amazing FACT

Many small desert mammals, such as gerbils, spend the day in burrows underground to avoid the scorching heat. Just 50 cm below ground, the temperature is 20 °C cooler. Gerbils' breathing keeps the burrow moist. To keep this moisture in, the burrow entrance is blocked with earth.

PRAIRIE DOG TOWN

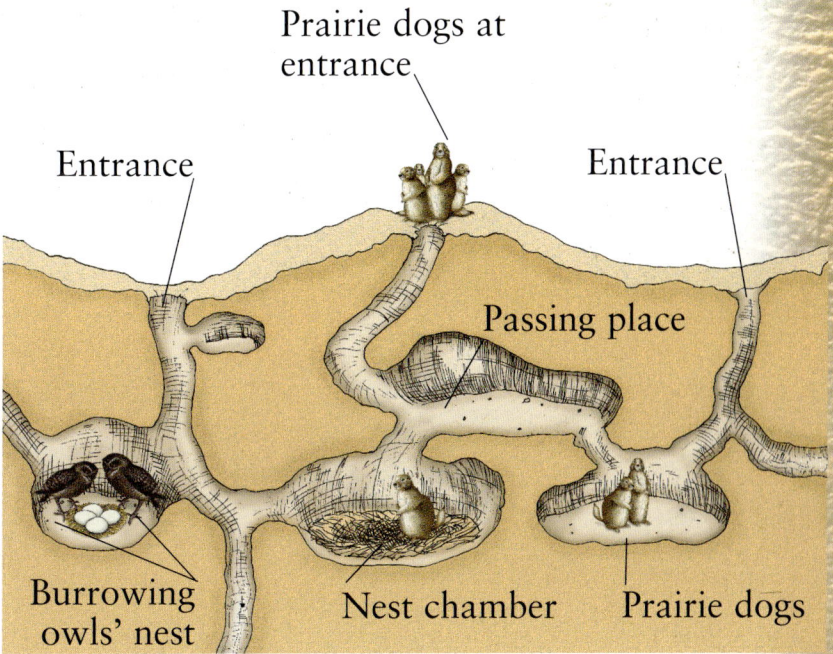

Prairie dogs at entrance

Entrance

Entrance

Passing place

Burrowing owls' nest

Nest chamber

Prairie dogs

Prairie dogs are rabbit-sized rodents from the grasslands of North America. Thousands live together in vast, inter-connected systems of burrows, called 'towns'. Each town has many tunnels and chambers, with several entrance holes and escape hatches. Mounds of soil are piled up around each hole to draw in fresh air for ventilation. Burrowing owls often make their nests in deserted chambers.

9

Natural caves make excellent homes for many animals. They provide a warm, safe shelter, and are often used as nurseries for young. Some animals make their own cave-like dens in the ground or snow.

CAVE LIFE

Huge colonies of tiny birds called edible-nest swiftlets make their homes in vast caves in South-East Asia. They build their cup-shaped nests entirely from saliva, and use more saliva to stick them to the cave roof and walls.

Mexican free-tailed bats.

Amazing FACT

Many bats use caves as nurseries. In summer, Bracken Cave in Texas, USA, is home to 20 million female Mexican free-tailed bats and their young. At night, the mother bats leave the cave to hunt. Incredibly, when they return, they are able to identify their own babies from the crowd by their squeaks.

Edible-nest swiftlets are now endangered as their nests are used to make bird's nest soup. It takes two nests to make a bowl of soup. Collectors risk their lives to get these valuable nests from mountain caves.

Cave fish have adapted to life under the ground by becoming colourless and blind. In the dark, they do not need to see colours or be colourful.

DENS FOR BEARS

As winter approaches and food becomes scarce, bears hibernate in snug, warm dens in ready-made caves, inside hollow trees or among piles of rocks. They stay in their dens for six months or more, until spring comes. During this time, the bears live off stores of fat which they have accumulated (collected in their bodies) during the autumn. The den provides a safe, warm place for their cubs to be born during the winter.

POLAR BEAR DEN

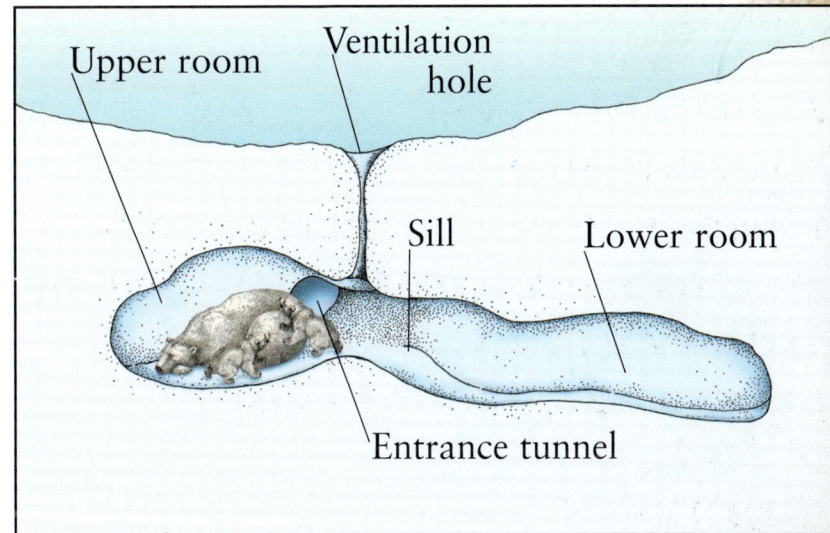

In October, a female polar bear digs a den in the snow. The den consists of a tunnel several metres long, leading to an oval-shaped chamber. An air hole in the roof allows stale air to escape. Her cubs are born here in December or January. They grow rapidly on their mother's rich milk and are ready to leave their ice house in spring.

In spring, brown bears emerge from months of hibernation in their dens. Between now and the following autumn, they roam large areas, travelling long distances in the search for food.

Beavers live in North America and Europe. They use their amazing building skills to create a home which will protect them from predators, such as bears, and where they can store food for the coming winter.

BUILDING A DAM

Firstly, the beavers build a dam across a river or stream. The dam is made from logs, branches, sticks and stones. It is thickly plastered with mud to make it watertight. The dam holds the water back and creates a small, deep lake.

A beaver's teeth are its main tools for felling trees for building. Its large, sharp front teeth are shaped like chisels and are ideal for cutting. It takes just a few minutes to bite through a thick stem.

Beavers are constantly inspecting the dam to make sure that it is in good condition. Gaps are quickly plugged with mud and sticks to stop the dam from leaking.

Amazing FACT

Beavers' dams are extraordinary feats of engineering. The largest dam ever built is probably one across the Jefferson River in Montana, USA. It is 700 metres long and can bear the weight of a person riding across it on horseback. The American beaver has very strong jaws so that it can drag building materials to its dam.

An American beaver's dam.

Young beavers, or kits, are born in the lodge. They stay for two years before leaving to build their own.

THE LODGE

Next, the beavers build an island of logs, branches and bark several metres high in the middle of the lake. This is their lodge. Inside the lodge, they hollow out a living chamber. They cake or cover the chamber walls with mud to keep it warm.

BEAVERS' LODGE

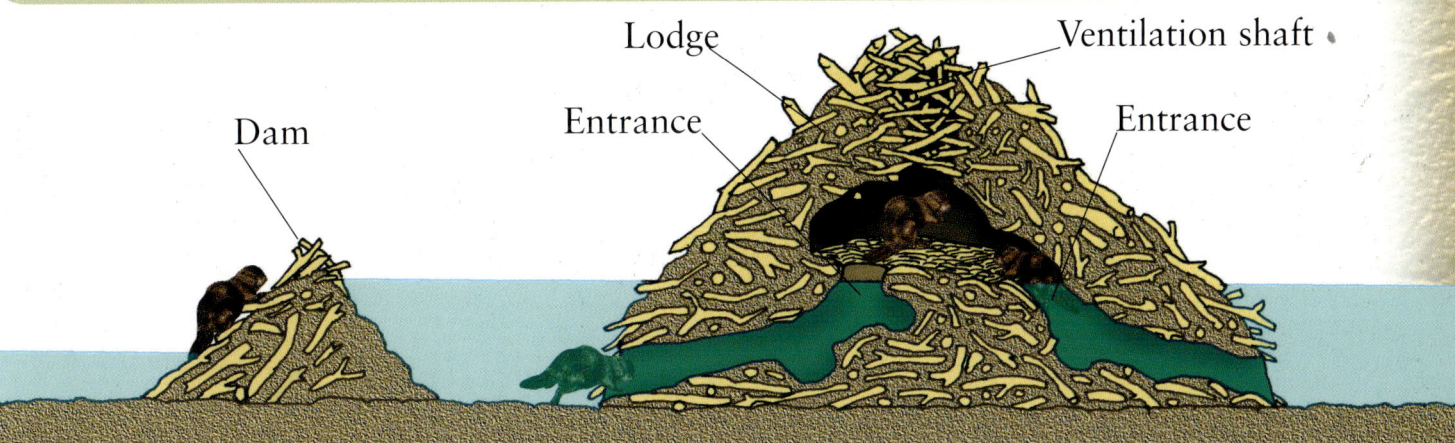

Lodge   Ventilation shaft
Entrance   Entrance
Dam

Lodges vary in shape and size but usually consist of a central chamber which acts as a living room and bedroom. The floor of the lodge is above water level.

The only way in is through a series of underwater passages. Nearby is a store of branches and stems for the beavers to feed on throughout the winter.

13

INSECT ARCHITECTS

Despite their small size, many insects are skilful architects. In particular, social insects such as ants, wasps and bees build elaborate nests, using paper, wax, leaves and mud, where they lay their eggs.

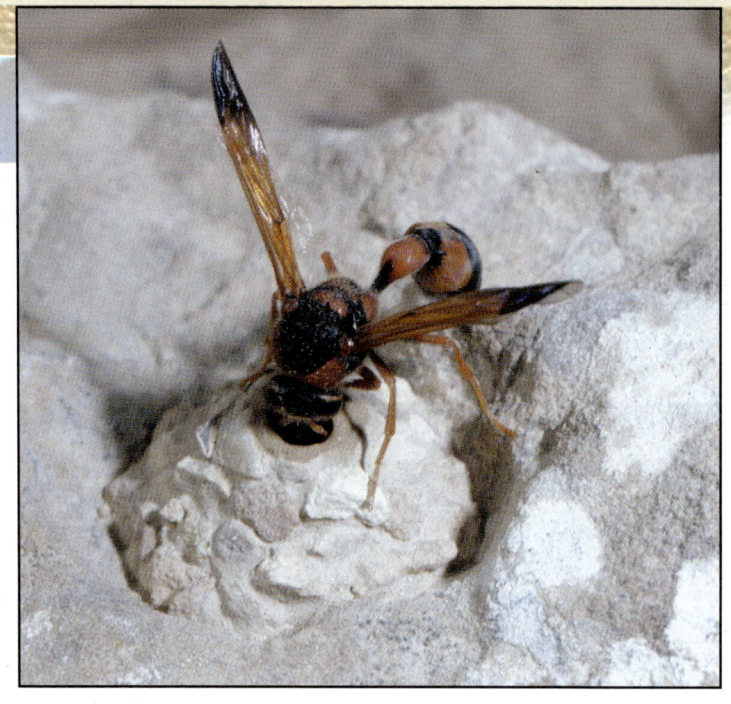

Potter wasps use tiny mud pellets to build pot-shaped nests for their eggs. The wasps stock their nests with half-dead insects for the grubs to feed on when they hatch.

TINY TAILORS

Green tree ants from Australia build their oval-shaped nests from leaves which are still attached to the trees. Some ants pull the edges of the leaves together with their legs. Others fetch ant grubs which they then use as sewing needles.

The ants pass the grubs from leaf edge to leaf edge, squeezing them so that they produce strands of sticky silk thread. The grubs make silk in glands in their mouths.

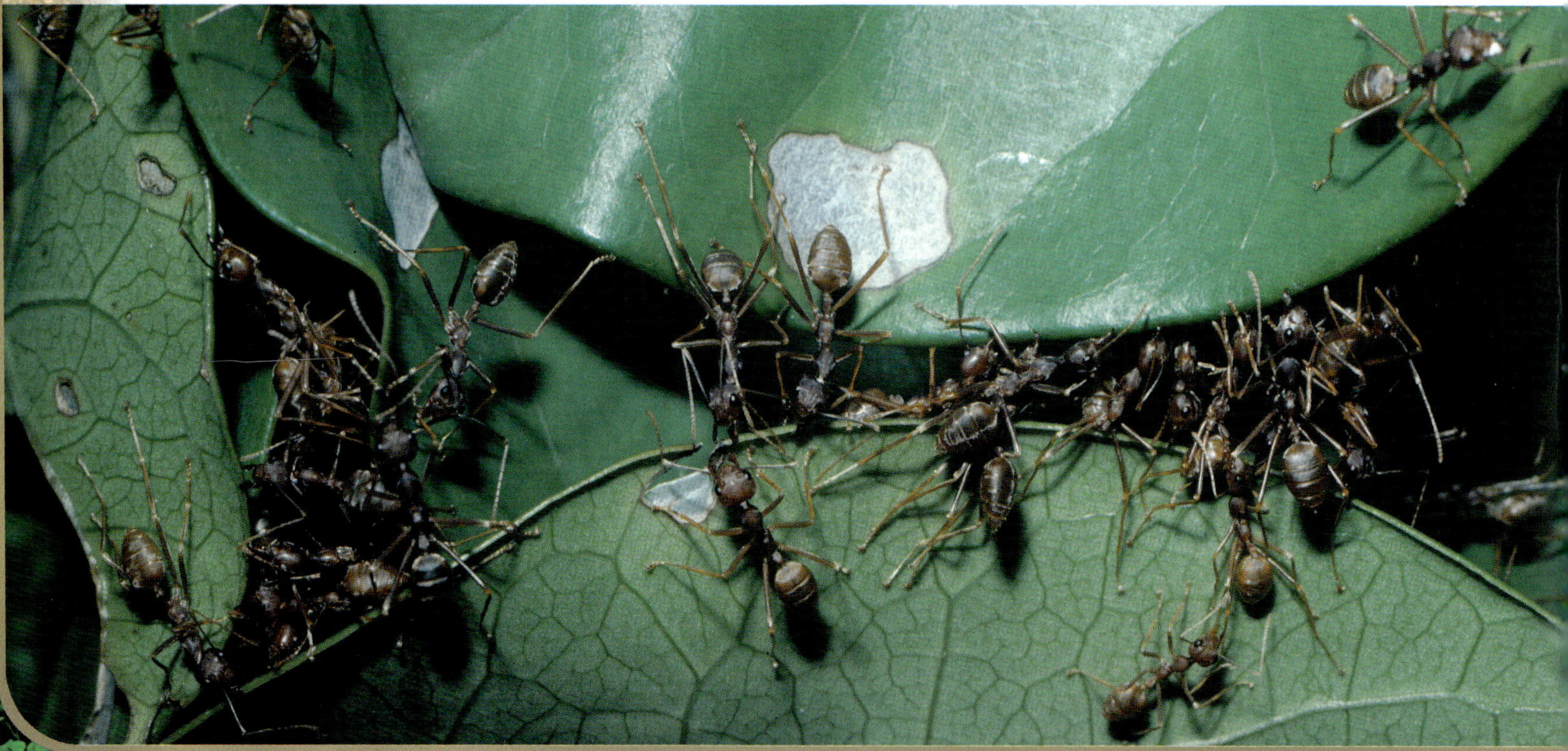

Amazing FACT

The silk that people use to make material comes from the cocoons of silk moth caterpillars. A caterpillar spins a silk case around itself when it is ready to change into an adult. An astonishing 3–4 kilometres of silk thread may be used to make a single cocoon.

Silk moth caterpillar and cocoon.

Some wasps build nests from paper. They make this paper from chewed up wood and saliva. The soggy pulp hardens as it dries. The paper is very strong and can be used to construct globe-shaped nests 1 metre wide.

BEEHIVE BUILDERS

Thousands of honeybees live in large swarms. The bees make wax in special glands underneath their abdomens. Using their legs, they shape this wax into six-sided cells. Incredibly, the cells are always the same size and shape, and their walls are the same thickness. The bees build rows of cells to form a honeycomb.

Some cells contain eggs laid by the queen bee. Others are used to store honey and pollen to feed the newly-hatched grubs. The cells are then covered with wax lids.

15

Some of the most amazing of all animal homes are the towering mud nests built by tiny insects called termites.

JOBS AND WORKERS

Termites live in colonies many millions strong. Different groups of termites have different jobs to do. The king and queen termite spend their lives breeding. It is the tiny worker termites who are responsible for building the nest. They are blind and each one is only about as big as a grain of rice.

Some types of termite live inside trees and house timbers where they cause a lot of damage. They chew their way through wood, digesting it as they go.

The strong, hard mud walls of the nest protect against predators, which try to raid the nest to feed on the termites.

INSIDE A TERMITE MOUND

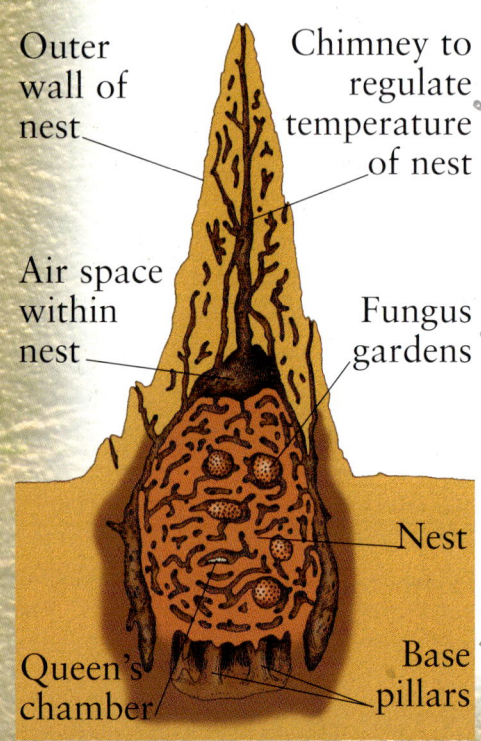

Outer wall of nest

Chimney to regulate temperature of nest

Air space within nest

Fungus gardens

Nest

Queen's chamber

Base pillars

The main part of the nest lies underground, below the mud tower. Here a maze of passages leads to various chambers. The king and queen live in the largest chamber, where the queen lays her eggs. Some are used as nurseries for the termite grubs. Other chambers are gardens where the termites grow fungi for food.

BUILDING A NEST

The workers construct the nest from particles of soil and mud which they dig up from the ground. They chew the soil with saliva to make a type of concrete which sets as hard as rock. Keeping the nest at the right temperature is essential, so it has its own ingenious air-conditioning system. Narrow channels running through the walls allow warm, stale air to escape and let cool, fresh air in.

Hollow chimneys of termite nests make an ideal home for dwarf mongooses. A medium-sized tower has plenty of room for a family of ten.

A termite nest in Africa.

Amazing FACT

In proportion to their size, termites build the largest structures of any land animals. The tallest termite nests are made by African termites. A mound discovered in Zaire stood nearly 13 metres high, as big as six tall humans. It measured just 3 metres around its base.

17

NESTING BIRDS

Many birds build nests as safe places to lay their eggs and raise their chicks. Birds choose their nest sites carefully to offer the best protection from predators. Nightingales, for example, nest in thick bushes to keep their eggs well hidden.

The world's smallest nests are built by hummingbirds. They may be no bigger than hazelnuts. The birds use cobwebs to fix their delicate nests to a twig.

KEEPING WARM

Birds' nests vary enormously. One of the most unusual nests is the huge mound of earth and plants built by the mallee fowl. The nest is built on the ground and can reach 4 metres high and 10 metres across.

The female mallee fowl lays her eggs inside the mound. Heat from the Sun and from the rotting plants keeps the eggs warm until they hatch about three months later.

Hornbill passing food into a nest.

Amazing FACT

Hornbills have an extraordinary way of keeping their eggs safe from predators. The female lays her eggs in a hole in a hollow tree trunk. Then the male and female seal up the entrance with lumps of soft mud. For the next few weeks, the male passes food to his mate through a tiny slit in the wall.

MAKING NESTS

There are two stages in making a nest – collecting materials and then construction. Birds may make thousands of trips to gather materials, which have three main functions – insulation, support and camouflage. Birds use natural materials when possible, including sticks, plants, feathers and moss. To build a simple cup nest, a bird puts the materials in place, then sits in the middle. It turns its body round, pressing the nest into shape.

1   2   3   4   5

Using his beak and feet, a male weaver bird constructs an amazing nest. Firstly, he tears off long strips of grass, and twists them around two twigs (1). He ties knots to hold them in place. Then he weaves in more strips to form a ring (2). As he continues to weave, the nest takes its ball shape (3 and 4). Finally, he adds a tube-like entrance (5). This makes it difficult for snakes to crawl inside and steal the eggs.

Sociable weaver birds build huge communal nests in the trees. They share the same roof and framework, but have a hundred or more separate nests beneath.

19

Birds, bees and termites are not the only animals that build nests. Many other creatures use nests as safe places to sleep or as nurseries for their eggs and young.

SLEEPING QUARTERS

Every night, an adult chimpanzee builds a nest for sleeping in. It chooses a secure base in the fork of a tree and bends down the nearby branches to make a mattress. A few leafy twigs make its bed more comfortable.

Grey tree frogs build their nest on a branch above a pond. They whip mucus into a soapy foam, and lay their eggs inside it. When the tadpoles hatch, they drop down into the water.

Adult chimpanzees have their own sleeping nests, although babies sleep with their mothers.

Water spiders live in ditches and ponds in a balloon-like nest filled with air. The nest is held in place by silk threads spun between the plants.

NURSERY NESTS

In the summer breeding season, mice and other small mammals build nursery nests for their young. A female harvest mouse builds her nest high among the tall stalks of grass or corn. Leaving the blades attached to their stalks, she shreds them into strips. Then she weaves them into a tight ball-shaped nest and lines it with feathers and down for warmth.

Like harvest mice, a dormouse builds a nursery nest in summer. It also makes a winter nest, in a tree stump or a burrow, where it hibernates for seven months.

Amazing FACT

In the rainforests of South America, some bats build daytime shelters out of large leaves. They chew away at the ends of a leaf's central rib so that the leaf drops down like tent flaps on each side. The bats roost underneath, clinging on to the rib with their back feet.

Tent-making bat.

Many animals that live underwater have no fixed homes. Instead, they find places to sleep and hide in the seabed sand, among rocks and seaweed, or on coral reefs.

REEF LIVING

Coral reefs are the richest habitats on Earth, home to thousands of fish and sea creatures who can all find food on the reef. Because a coral reef is such a crowded place, life is carefully balanced between nocturnal and daytime creatures. They take turns to hide and rest in caves and holes in the coral.

Fan worms build hard tubes round their soft bodies. They spread out their fan-like tentacles to filter food. If danger comes, they hide in their tubes.

By day, an octopus hides in its den among the coral. From the outside, the only sign of the den is a small crack. At night, the octopus emerges to feed.

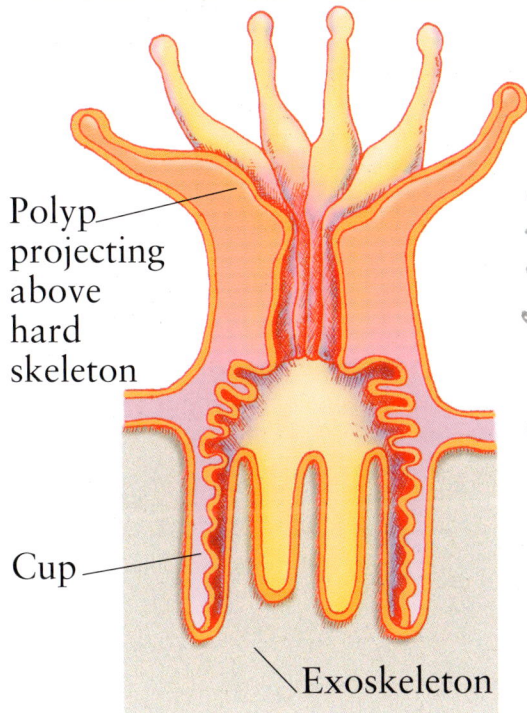

Polyp projecting above hard skeleton

Cup

Exoskeleton

Coral reefs are built by huge colonies of tiny sea creatures, called polyps, related to jellyfish and sea anemones. They extract chemicals from the sea water and use them to build stony, cup-like cases around their soft bodies. When the polyps die, the cases are left behind and gradually build up to form a reef.

Living coral.

DEEP-SEA DRILLING

Many seashore creatures take shelter by digging burrows in the soft sand. They include clams, cockles and razorshells. Some are even able to drill holes in solid rock. The piddock, a small mollusc, grips a rock with its sucker-like foot. Then it twists and turns its shell to bore a deep hole into the rock.

Amazing FACT

At night, a parrot fish secretes a bubble of mucus around its body. This sleeping bag takes about half an hour to make and half an hour to break out of in the morning. It may keep the parrot fish safe by stopping its smell reaching its enemies, such as moray eels.

Lugworms live in L-shaped burrows on seashores. As they burrow, they feed on grains of sand, extracting any goodness and pushing waste up into a coiled cast.

A parrot fish in its sleeping bag.

23

Some animals do not have their homes to themselves. Their nests, burrows and shells attract lodgers. These lodgers take advantage of a ready-made shelter, whether the home-owners like it or not.

Amazing FACT
Hermit crabs do not have their own shells. To protect their soft bodies, they lodge in empty mollusc shells. As they grow, they simply find larger shells. Hermit crabs do not live alone. Many carry sea anemones on their shells. The anemones' stinging tentacles protect them from predators.

After laying her egg, the cuckoo flies away. She leaves the foster parents to raise her chick. The young cuckoo may push the other chicks out of the nest so that it has more food for itself.

Shearwater birds nest in cliff-top tunnels, sharing their homes with tuatara lizards. The tuataras clear the tunnels for when the birds return from sea to lay their eggs.

CUCKOO IN THE NEST

Building a nest is time-consuming work. So cuckoos do not bother to make their own. Instead, a female cuckoo lays her single egg in another bird's nest. For disguise, the cuckoo's egg usually has similar markings and colouring to the other eggs. This stops the host bird spotting it and throwing it out. Sometimes, cuckoo chicks even throw the other chicks out of the nest.

A hermit crab and sea anemone.

SAFE AS HOUSES

Sometimes a lodger can be very useful to a home-owner. Clownfish live among the waving, poisonous tentacles of sea anemones, where they are safe from predators. In return, they attract other fish which swim towards the anemones. Then the anemones catch these fish for food. The clownfish may also help to keep the anemones healthy by cleaning bits of waste and dead skin off them.

Clownfish do not get stung because the slime covering their bodies lacks a special type of chemical. In most fish, it is this chemical which causes the anemones' stings to discharge their painful poison.

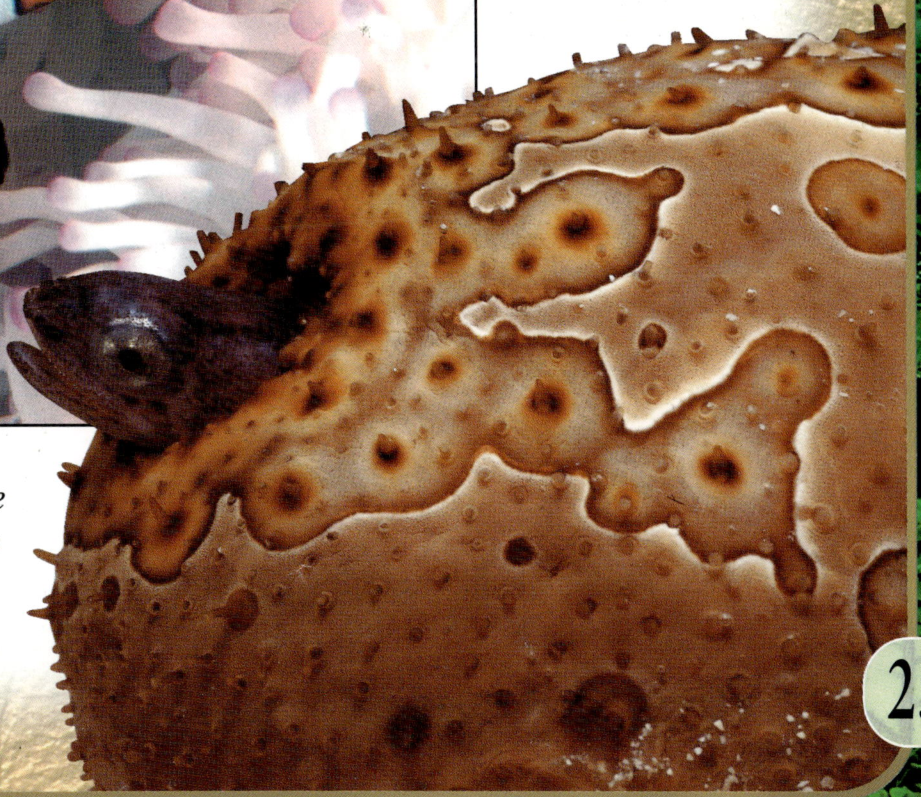

A pearlfish finds a safe hideaway inside the body of a sea cucumber. It wriggles in, head first, then rests inside with its head poking out. Sometimes, it even starts to eat away at the sea cucumber from the inside.

Wherever they live, animals need basic essentials to survive. Some keep a particular patch of land, called a territory, which provides them with everything they need – food, a safe place to rest, and a place to mate and raise their young.

TERRITORY TYPES

Some territories cover hundreds of square kilometres. Others may not be much bigger than their owners. Territories may be held by a single animal, a pair, a family group or even a whole herd or swarm. Whatever type of territory it is, its owner guards it fiercely (see pages 28–29).

A dragonfly's territory is a stretch of riverbank which it defends fiercely. It flies up and down, on patrol, looking out for insect prey and unwelcome visitors.

Some animals only need a temporary territory. In spring, male sticklebacks find somewhere to build a nest. Then they attract a female to lay her eggs in it.

PUTTING ON A DISPLAY

Some animals use territories solely for attracting mates for breeding. Each year, male sage grouse establish special sites called leks where they perform courtship displays. Females gather around the edges to watch. They choose the most impressive male as their mate, often the male with the best, most central site.

Pandas usually feed at dawn and dusk.

TIGER TERRITORY

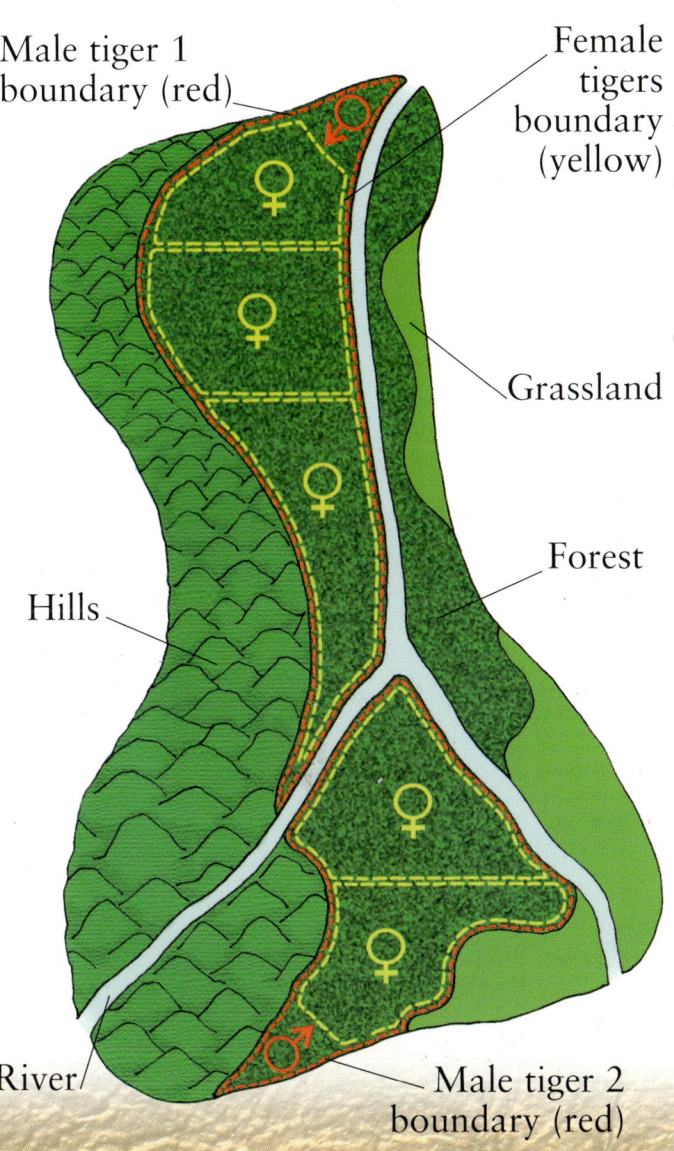

Male tiger 1 boundary (red)

Female tigers boundary (yellow)

Grassland

Forest

Hills

River

Male tiger 2 boundary (red)

Tigers are solitary hunters who patrol their own territory and defend it against other tigers. The diagram on the left shows the arrangement of several tiger territories in Chitwan National Park in Nepal. Each male tiger has a large territory, about three to four times bigger than a female's patch. These do not overlap with each other but contain several smaller female territories. A territory must contain prey, pools for drinking from and shady trees for resting in.

A tiger marks the boundaries of its territory by spraying strong-smelling urine on trees, bushes and rocks. An average male tiger's territory covers about 80 square kilometres.

Animals go to great lengths to safeguard their territories and their precious resources. To warn off intruders and show ownership, animals use a variety of visual displays, smells and sounds.

FIGHTING TALK

Many animals defend their territories against others of the same species. This avoids direct competition for food and shelter. Fighting is a risky business, so some animals make threatening gestures instead. If these do not work, a real fight may break out.

Indri lemurs use loud howls and songs to warn intruders away from the boundaries of their rainforest territory.

Male hippos warn off rival males from their riverbank territories by opening their mouths to display big canine teeth.

Amazing FACT

A sea anemone's tiny territory is a patch of rock. An anemone carefully chooses a suitable spot where food is easy to catch. Anemones are savage, despite their size. If a rival anemone appears, the territory owner uses its stinging tentacles to fight it off.

Sea anemones fighting.

WARNING SIGNALS

Other warning signals include strong smells, loud calls and visual messages. Some animals use dung, urine or strong body scents to mark their territorial boundaries. Intruders recognise the scent and stay away. Other animals display bright colours as a warning. In thick undergrowth or forest colours are difficult to see, so animals use loud, far-reaching calls and songs.

A robin puffs up its bright red breast feathers to warn other robins to stay away. Robins also sing to advertise their ownership of a patch of woodland.

Guillemots live in crowded cliff-top colonies. To protect their nest-ledge, they use threat displays.

29

Biggest coral reef

• The biggest coral reef in the world is the Great Barrier Reef off the north-east coast of Australia. It stretches for 2028 kilometres and covers an area of more than 200,000 square kilometres.

Largest sea shell

• Giant clams live on coral reefs and grow record-breaking shells. Their shells can measure more than 1 metre in length.

Best burrowers

• Mole rats are brilliant burrowers. Using their teeth to dig through the soil, they can shift 50 times their own body weight.

Colossal colonies

• About 100 years ago, a prairie dog town in Texas, in the USA, was estimated to be home to a staggering 400 million animals.

Enormous nests

• The biggest birds' nest on record was built by a pair of bald eagles in Florida, USA. It measured almost 3 metres across and 6 metres deep. It weighed 3 tonnes.

Smallest nests

• Tiny hummingbirds build the smallest birds' nests. A bee hummingbird's nest is thimble-sized and a vervain hummingbird's nest is only half as big as a walnut shell.

Strangest nest

• Some birds use strange building materials. A white stork's nest in France was made from hats, shoes, stockings, buttons and leather.

In a hole

• The devil's hole pupfish is only found in part of an underground pool in the middle of the baking hot Nevada Desert, in the USA.

GLOSSARY

camouflage
Special colourings or markings which help to hide an animal or its home, protecting it from enemies.

cocoons
The silk cases which insect grubs spin around their bodies when they are ready to turn into adults.

endangered
Animals which are in danger of becoming extinct, or dying out.

glands
Parts of an animal's body which produce chemicals or substances.

grubs
Worm-like young of an insect.

habitats
The type of place an animal lives in, such as rainforest or desert.

hibernate
A time of inactivity or deep sleep during the winter. Animals hibernate to save energy.

insulation
Using materials to keep in warmth.

leks
Temporary territories used by some birds during the breeding season.

nocturnal
Animals that sleep by day and are active at night.

predators
Animals that hunt and kill other animals, called prey, for food.

social insects
Insects that live together in colonies or groups, and rely on each other for survival.

species
A group of living things that are grouped together because they have similar features.

territories
Areas or patches of land which provide animals with food and a safe place to rest.